MEXICAN RIVIERA
portrait of a place

MEXICAN RIVIERA

portrait of a place

CLIFF AND NANCY HOLLENBECK

GRAPHIC ARTS BOOKS

Library of Congress Control Number: 2007929885
International Standard Book Number: 978-0-88240-696-1

Book compilation © 2007 by
Graphic Arts Books, an imprint of
Graphic Arts Center Publishing Company
P.O. Box 10306, Portland, Oregon 97296-0306
503/226-2402; www.gacpc.com

The five-dot logo is a registered trademark of
Graphic Arts Center Publishing Company.

President: Charles M. Hopkins
Associate Publisher: Douglas A. Pfeiffer
Editorial Staff: Timothy W. Frew, Kathy Howard, Jean Bond-Slaughter
Production Coordinator: Heather Doornink
Cover Design: Elizabeth Watson
Interior Design: Jean Andrews

Printed in the United States of America

FRONT COVER: ◗ Framed by palms and flowers,
the aptly named Dreams Beach is a popular place in Puerto Vallarta.
BACK COVER: ◗ A world-famous Acapulco cliff diver is silhouetted against the setting sun.
◄◄ Golden sand and sunshine are the main elements that make beaches along Puerto
Vallarta's Bahía de Banderas (which translates as "Bay of Flags") so welcoming.
◄ Looking like a city of carnival lights, Acapulco comes alive at night.
► Mazatlán is famous for its gorgeous, colorful sunsets that sweep
across the sky and make dusk walks along the
beach an unforgettable experience.

◄ Folkloric ribbon dancers perform at the Westin Resort
in Puerto Vallarta, Jalisco State, birthplace of mariachi music.
▲ Gentle surf and a golden sunset sweep across the
rocks at Ixtapa's Vista Hermosa Beach.

◄ The Pedregal residential area of
Cabo San Lucas looks out to the city and marina
below, along with a beautiful view of Cabo San Lucas Bay.
▲ Pots of colorful bougainvilleas are common in homes
and resorts along the Mexican Riviera.

◄ The pristine beach resort area Playa Azul,
or "Blue Beach," runs along the Bay of Manzanillo.
▲ A friendly salesman shows off silver jewelry and handwoven
blankets in his small shop in San José del Cabo.

▲ Gentle breezes make the
palms sway on the beach at Palmilla
near San José del Cabo.

▲ Sitting beside a private casita pool at
Las Brisas Resort, empty loungers are framed by
palms and Acapulco Bay in the distance.

▲ The San José del Cabo Cathedral, originally built in
1730, overlooks the main plaza and is the heart of this lovely city.
▶ A couple launches their catamaran to sail toward the
wildlife sanctuary Isla de Pájaros, "Island of Birds,"
across from the beaches of Mazatlán.

◄ Footsteps lead into the sunrise along the Pacific
Ocean, on Finisterra Beach, at Land's End, Cabo San Lucas.
Land's End is the southernmost point of Baja California,
where the Pacific Ocean and the Sea of Cortés meet.
▲ Waves from the Sea of Cortés crash into rocks
along the deserted Palmilla Beach.

17

▲ Young boys play in Pacific Ocean
surf on the beach at Land's End, Cabo San Lucas.
► A small water taxi waits to take tourists to one of the remote
beaches near Cabo San Lucas, or to give a guided tour of the bay.
►► The wide stretch of golden sand, set along the Pacific Ocean,
at Land's End, Cabo San Lucas, is called Divorce Beach,
although it is very popular with newlyweds.

◄ A lone pelican flies over a palm-thatched *palapa* on Palmilla Beach, set on
the Sea of Cortés, between the cities of Cabo San Lucas and San Jose del Cabo.
▲ A beachcomber takes a moment to watch as a migratory gray whale spouts
just offshore in the waters of the Sea of Cortés near Cabo San Lucas.
►► A *panga*, a small tour boat, heads toward El Arco, "the Arch,"
the most commonly used image to represent Cabo San Lucas.

▲ Pelicans looking for a fresh catch circle a fishing
boat returning from a successful day on the Sea of Cortés.
▶ Golfers play at the Cabo del Sol course, by the Sea of Cortés at San José del Cabo.
▶▶ Flipping his tail in the sunset, a migratory gray whale spouts
in the Sea of Cortés, near San José del Cabo.

◄ Plying Mexico's famous straw hats,
a lovely young beach vendor flashes her smile
at passing tourists on the beaches of Cabo San Lucas.
▲ A speedboat pulls an adventurous tourist strapped to a
colorful parasail over the Bahía (bay) of Cabo San Lucas.

▲ A beautiful dusk is seen from the view at Di Giorgio,
a restaurant and bar near Cabo San Lucas, as it settles across
the Sea of Cortés and the extended rock formation of Land's End.

▶ In Mazatlán, *palapas* sit along this gorgeous stretch of sand
called Sabalo Beach, looking to the outcropping
rock formation of Punta del Sabalo.

◄ A tourist enjoys the view of El Faro Bay
and El Faro Lighthouse, the southern point of Mazatlán.
▲ Thatched *palapas* and a catamaran frame swimmers near Playa
Mazatlán, with Isla de Venados (Deer Island) in the distance.

◄ Waiting for a sunbather to return from
the Pacific Ocean waves, a beach chair sits on
the sand along Mazatlán's popular Golden Zone.
▲ Striking pink hibiscus are found along the walkways
and resort areas of the Mexican Riviera.

▲ The city of Mazatlán gleams in the background, as a
couple walks beside the ocean surf on Torres Mazatlán Beach.
▶ The renovated, stately Angela Peralta Theater, in
Mazatlán's Old Town, was built in the 1870s.

◄ Regular performances in Mazatlán
feature flying Totonac Indians who swing
from ropes tied to their ankles, as a fifth man
stands atop the fifty-foot tower playing a musical drum.
▲ The Cafe Pacifico, located in the center of Mazatlán's
Old Town, is a popular gathering place.

▲ Laden with colorful baskets, a vender sells
his merchandise along Mazatlán's inviting beaches.
▶ Mazatlán Cathedral, with its twin golden towers and
stately bandstand, is the heart of the city.

▲ A sombrero-topped
iguana poses for tourist photos.
► Colorful fishing boats sit idle in the
afternoon sun along the city of Mazatlán's
Playa Olas Atlas, or "Big Waves," Beach.

◄ A majestic float carries one of Mazatlán's beauty queens, in
the city's biggest fiesta, Carnival, an annual February celebration.
▲ In the city of Mazatlán, a daughter peeks at passing tourists,
as her Indian mother sells appealing handmade dolls.

▲ Beach chairs are waiting along Puerto
Vallarta's Playa Camarones, "Shrimps Beach,"
with golden sand and warm Pacific Ocean waves.
▶ A baby giant sea turtle is released into the
Pacific Ocean near Puerto Vallarta.

◄ This viewpoint, looking at Puerto Vallarta and the
Bahía de Banderas, is found along the Malecon city walkway.
▲ Slightly south of Puerto Vallarta, this dramatic entryway leads
to the gorgeous Careyes Playa, "Turtle Beach," Resort.

▲ The walkway along Puerto Vallarta's
Malecon is a great place to people watch and
to enjoy both the city and the view of the bay.
▶ Artists' paintings are displayed along the
walkway of Puerto Vallarta's Malecon.

◄ Puerto Vallarta is a gorgeous mix of red rooftops, the
beautiful cathedral, and Bahía de Banderas, "Bay of Flags."
▲ Blankets, plates, pots, and bags are for sale in Puerto Vallarta.
►► A tourist couple takes a quiet horseback ride on Playa de Oro,
"Golden Beach," and enjoys a colorful Puerto Vallarta sunset.

55

▲ Hot red hibiscus contrast with the bright blue sky.
▶ This lovely and tranquil arched doorway is part of a
suite at Las Alamandas Resort, located
just south of Puerto Vallarta.

◀ Sun and fun greet this happy little
Mexican girl on Puerto Vallarta's Dreams Beach.
▲ A Mexican *vaquero*, "cowboy," stands with his horse
on Revolcadero Beach, south of Acapulco.

▲ Playa de Oro, with its many restaurants and sunbathing facilities, is a favorite destination with Puerto Vallarta tourists.

▶ *Caballeo del Mar* (which translates as "Seahorse") is a nine-foot-high bronze statue created by Rafael Zamarripa. It was the first sculpture set along the Malecon in 1976.

◄ Tourists shop for artwork in Puerto Vallarta's *zócalo*,
"main square," with the cathedral in the background.
▲ A young Mexican woman plays the guitar at a
villa along the Mexican Riviera.

▲ Tourists play along the huge
expanse of beach at Punta Mita, "Point
of Simple Pleasures," just north of Puerto Vallarta.
▶ Our Lady of Guadalupe Cathedral, with its distinctive
crown and clock tower, is a beautiful Puerto Vallarta landmark.
▶▶ Boats in the Manzanilla marina at Playa San Pedrito
are silhouetted in the evening dusk light.

◄ Tourists bask in the sun
around Manzanillo's Karmina Palace pool.
▲ A young Mexican girl sells pealed mangos, sprinkled
with hot pepper sauce, along the beaches.

▲ Popular rental jet skis wait near the waters of
Playa Salahua at Manzanillo's Karmina Palace Resort.
▶ In Manzanillo, a young Mexican girl plays in the waters
of Lagoon Penatis, next to Playa Miramar.

◄ The entry steps to a private villa suite at
Las Hadas Resort in Manzanillo seem to climb into the sky.
▲ A private palm-thatched villa overlooks
Santiago Bay near Manzanillo.

◄ The Central Plaza fountain of
Manzanillo glows in the evening light.
▲ A Mexican mother and daughter enjoy an
ear of roasted corn in the warm sunset.

▲ The Pacific Ocean, Playa Linda,
or "Beautiful Beach," and the vibrant
jungle meet just north of Ixtapa.

▲ Zihuatanejo's lush green tropical jungle
runs from parts of the city up into the surrounding
mountains of Sierra Madre del Sur.

▲ The quiet pool area at
Zihuatanejo's Villa del Sol, "Home of
the Sun," Resort is very inviting.

▲ A couple strolls in the gentle Pacific Ocean surf, as it brushes against the towering pyramid-shaped Las Brisas Ixtapa Resort.

▲ Tourists enjoy jet-skiing in
the waters off Playa Las Gatas, "Cats Beach,"
located just across the bay from the city of Zihuatanejo.
▶ A fisherman carries his daily catch from the
Bay of Zihuatanejo up the main beach.

◄ In Zihuatanejo the sun sets through waving palms,
as a tourist walks along Playa La Ropa, "Beach of Clothing."
▲ Throughout the Mexican Riviera, visitors follow signs such
as this one to find their way to a *playa* or "beach."

▲ A carved and painted wooden
mask seems to keep an eye on Madeira
Beach in the village of Zihuatanejo.

▲ Tourist souvenirs and handmade treasures
are displayed for sale at an Ixtapa Village gift shop.
►► Los Moros Island, in the Pacific Ocean, is silhouetted
against a brilliant sun setting just off the coast of Ixtapa.

◄ A late afternoon look through the *palapas* at
Acapulco's Playa Icacos Beach shows that sunbathers
have left for the restaurants and evening entertainment.
▲ The exciting city of Acapulco shines in the afternoon
sun, while bougainvillea flowers frame the view
of Bahía de Acapulco, the "Bay of Acapulco."

▲ Acapulco's Nuestra Señora de la Soledad Cathedral
is distinguished by a mosque-like dome and Byzantine towers.
► Isla de la Roqueta, in the Pacific Ocean just west of Acapulco
Bay, is silhouetted in the late afternoon sun.

◄ The main *zócalo,* or "city square," of
Acapulco stands empty in the warm afternoon sun.
▲ Catamaran sailboats rest along Playa Hornos
as the day ends in Acapulco.

▲ A pool holds night light reflections
of the beautiful restaurant Club La Concha,
at Las Brisas Resort in Acapulco.

▲ Tourists take in the
sights of Acapulco and its bay,
onboard a rented jet ski.

▲ The golden warm sands of Playa Icacos are swept by the
waters of Acapulco Bay, showcasing the hotels that line its edge.
► Many colorful umbrellas dot beaches all along the Mexican Riviera.
►► Acapulco Bay reflects the brilliant night lights of the
city across a casita pool at Las Brisas Resort.

◄ A look across the *palapas* displays a
quiet Icacos Beach, Acapulco's main tourist beach.
▲ Acapulco's Caleta Beach is popular with sunbathers
and aficionados of good local seafood.

▲ High-rise resorts overlook the
afternoon blue waters of Acapulco Bay.
▶ A couple takes a sunset walk, after a horseback
ride, along the huge expanse of Revolcadero
Beach just south of Acapulco.

◄ Just south of Acapulco, Puerto Marquis
is a popular, yet less-crowded, beach area.
▲ Acapulco cliff divers make their evening parade
to the cliffside at La Quebrada, lighted
by the flame of their torches.

▲ An Acapulco cliff diver makes a
hundred-foot leap at La Quebrada, just northwest
of town. *La quebrada* means "broken one" in Spanish.
▶ Silhouetted against a brilliant Mexican sunset, an
Acapulco cliff diver flies through the air above
a rocky coast along the Pacific Ocean.

▲ Palms and sunset reflect
in a still, small lagoon next to
Palamar Beach in Ixtapa.

▲ A couple takes a leisurely
afternoon stroll on the wide golden sands
at Hacienda del Mar Beach, near Cabo San Lucas.
▶▶ A seagull flies by as the sun sets in a blinding
orange splash across Land's End and the
gentle waters of the Sea of Cortés.